# GRAMMAR in use

## REFERENCE AND PRACTICE
## FOR INTERMEDIATE STUDENTS
## OF ENGLISH

### Answer Key

# RAYMOND MURPHY
## with Roann Altman

### Consultant: William E. Rutherford

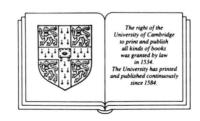

The right of the
University of Cambridge
to print and publish
all kinds of books
was granted by law
in 1534.
The University has printed
and published continuously
since 1584.

## Cambridge University Press
Cambridge
New York ■ Port Chester
Melbourne ■ Sydney

MURPHY ANSWER

Published by the Press Syndicate of the University of Cambridge
The Pitt Building, Trumpington Street, Cambridge CB2 1RP
40 West 20th Street, New York, NY 10011, USA
10 Stamford Road, Oakleigh, Melbourne 3166, Australia

© Cambridge University Press 1989

First published 1989
Third printing 1990

Printed in the United States of America

*Library of Congress Cataloging-in-Publication Data*

Murphy, Raymond.
Grammar in use.
Contents: [1] Student's book – [2] Answer key.
1. English language – Textbooks for foreign speakers.
2. English language – Grammar – 1950 –
3. English language – United States.  I. Altman, Roann.
II. Title.
PE1128.M775  1989        428.2′4        88-29951

ISBN 0 521 34843 9 Student's Book: paperback
ISBN 0 521 35701 2 Answer Key: paperback

# Answer Key

This Answer Key gives the answers to all the exercises in the Student's Book to *Grammar in Use*. It is useful for self-study and as a handy reference for teachers.

In these answers, sometimes the full form of the verb is given (e.g., "I am, it is, she will, he has," etc.) and sometimes the short form (e.g., "I'm, it's, she'll, he's," etc.). Often it doesn't matter which you choose. But see Appendix 4 in the Student's Book for details of when short forms are not possible.

---

## Unit 1

**1.1**
1. am trying
2. is snowing
3. are you looking
4. are making
5. am looking
6. Are you enjoying
7. are yelling
8. are you wearing
9. am not working
10. am not eating

**1.2**
1. is rising / is falling / is increasing
2. is getting
3. is getting / is becoming
4. is changing
5. is rising / is increasing
6. is improving (*or* is getting better)
7. is getting / is becoming

**1.3**
2. am working
3. Are you enjoying
4. am not working
5. am building
6. Are you doing
7. are helping

---

## Unit 2

**2.1**
1. opens . . . closes
2. do the banks close
3. don't use
4. do you smoke
5. do you do
6. does your father come . . . comes
7. takes . . . does it take
8. play . . . don't play
9. does "deceive" mean

**2.2**
1. The sun doesn't rise in the west. It rises in the east.
2. Mice don't catch cats. Cats catch mice.
3. Carpenters don't make things from metal. They make things from wood.
4. The Amazon River doesn't flow into the Pacific Ocean. It flows into the Atlantic Ocean.

**2.3**
1. How often does Ann watch television?
2. How often do you write to your parents?
3. What time do you usually have dinner (in the evening)?
4. Where does Tom work?
5. How often do you go to the movies?
6. Why do people do stupid things?
7. How often does the car break down?

# Unit 3

**3.1**
1  right
2  wrong – are they talking
3  wrong – Do you believe
4  wrong – is trying
5  right
6  wrong – What do you think
7  right
8  wrong – I usually go

**3.2**
1  don't belong
2  is coming . . . don't want
3  flows
4  is flowing
5  Does it ever snow
6  grow . . . aren't growing
7  am learning
8  don't need
9  am getting
10  doesn't eat
11  don't believe
12  is staying . . . stays
13  live . . . do your parents live
14  is staying
15  does your father do . . . isn't working

# Unit 4

**4.1**
1  How long are you staying?
2  When are you leaving?
3  Are you going alone?
4  Are you going by car?
5  Where are you staying?

**4.2**
1  She is leaving next Friday.
2  She is staying in Hawaii for two weeks.
3  She is going with a friend of hers.
4  They are staying in a hotel.
5  They are going by plane.

**4.3**
1  I'm working late (till 9 p.m.).
2  I'm going to the theater with my mother.
3  I'm meeting Judy (at 8 p.m.).

**4.4**
1  are having
2  am not going . . . Are you going
3  starts
4  are getting
5  opens . . . closes
6  does the next train leave
7  are going . . . Are you coming

# Unit 5

**5.1**
1  I'm going to call him after lunch.
2  I'm going to have it in a little while.
3  Not yet. I'm going to paint it soon.
4  Not yet. I'm going to fix it this afternoon.

**5.2**
1  What are you going to wear?
2  Where is he going to hang it?
3  Who are you going to invite?

**5.3**
1  No, I was going to buy it, but I changed my mind.
2  No, she was going to get married, but she changed her mind.
3  No, he was going to quit (his job), but he changed his mind.
4  No, they were going to go to Greece (for their vacation), but they changed their minds.
5  No, I was going to play tennis, but I changed my mind.
6  No, I was going to invite her (to the party), but I changed my mind.

**5.4**
1  He is going to fail (his exams).
2  He is going to be late.
3  It is going to sink.
4  She/The car is going to run out of gas.

# Unit 6

**6.1**  1  I'll have / I'll get
2  I'll call / I'll phone / I'll telephone
3  I'll turn / I'll switch
4  I'll go
5  I'll do / I'll write
6  I'll have

**6.2**  1  I think I'll go to bed.
2  I think I'll walk.
3  I don't think I'll play tennis.
4  I don't think I'll go swimming.

**6.3**  1  I'll get dinner ready.
2  No, that's all right. I'll do the shopping.
3  No, that's all right. I'll water the plants.

**6.4**  1  B: Sure, I'll call you tonight.
B: Yes, I promise I'll call you tonight.
2  B: Okay, I'll fix it tomorrow.
A: Do you promise?
B: Yes, I promise I'll fix it tomorrow.
3  A: Do you promise?
B: Yes, I promise I won't tell anyone.
4  B: I won't hurt you.
A: Do you promise?
B: Yes, I promise I won't hurt you.

# Unit 7  These verb forms are more natural.

**7.1**  1  am going
2  will rain
3  will get
4  is coming
5  are going
6  won't hurt

**7.2**  2  Do you think she'll come?
3  What time do you think they'll arrive?
(*or* they'll come)
4  Do you think it'll rain?
5  How much do you think it'll cost?
6  Do you think they'll get married?
7  When do you think it'll finish?

**7.3**  1  She'll probably say nothing.
2  I bet she'll go to South America.
3  I think she'll leave tomorrow.
4  I suppose she'll go there by plane.
5  I think she'll be back quite soon.
6  Yes, I'm sure I'll miss her very much.

**7.4**  1  What time shall I call (you)?
2  What shall we have (for dinner)?
3  Shall we go by car or (shall we) walk?

# Unit 8

**8.1**  1  I'll get
2  I'm going to wash
3  are you going to paint
4  I'll call
5  it is going to fall
6  I'm going to buy
7  I'll show
8  I'll have
9  he is going to take . . . he is going to start
10  I'll do
11  we'll have
12  I'll go . . . I'm going to get . . . I'll get
13  I'll take . . . Toshi is going to take

# Unit 9

**9.1**   1   leave
2   will call . . . arrive
3   come ("police" is plural)
4   will be . . . passes
5   see . . . won't recognize
6   won't start . . . arrives
7   Will you be . . . am
8   need . . . will ask
9   will be . . . are

**9.2**   1   I'll give you my address when I find (*or* have found) somewhere to live.
2   Let's go out before it starts raining.

3   I'll come straight home after I do (*or* have done) the shopping.
4   You must come and see me when you're in Washington next month.
5   I'll get dinner ready when I finish (*or* have finished) reading this book.
6   We'll let you know as soon as we make (*or* have made) our decision.

**9.3**
| | | | |
|---|---|---|---|
| 1 | when | 5 | If |
| 2 | If | 6 | when |
| 3 | if | 7 | when |
| 4 | if | 8 | if |

# Unit 10

**10.1**   1   will be playing tennis.
2   will be studying.
3   we will be cleaning the apartment.

**10.2**   1   Bob was reading the newspaper.
2   He is reading the newspaper.
3   he will be reading the newspaper.

**10.3**   1   Will you be seeing Jean this afternoon?
2   Will you be using your typewriter tomorrow evening?
3   Will you be passing the post office while you're downtown?

**10.4**   1   Jim will have gone to bed.
2   he will have spent all his money.
3   she will have been in Canada exactly three years.

# Unit 11

**11.1**   1   she woke up early.
2   she walked to work.
3   she was late for work.
4   she had a sandwich for lunch.
5   she went out.
6   she slept very well.

**11.2**   1   taught
2   fell . . . hurt
3   sold
4   spent . . . bought . . . cost
5   threw . . . caught

**11.3**   1   How long did you stay there?
2   Did you stay in a hotel?
3   Did you go alone?
4   How did you travel?
5   Was the weather nice?
6   What did you do in the evenings?
7   Did you meet any interesting people?

**11.4**   1   didn't shave . . . didn't have
2   didn't eat . . . weren't
3   didn't rush . . . wasn't
4   wasn't . . . didn't understand

# Unit 12

**12.1**   2   was reading the newspaper.
3   she was cleaning her apartment.
4   she was having lunch.

5   she was washing some clothes.
6   she was watching TV.

**12.2**
1 was writing a letter in her room.
2 was getting ready to go out.
3 were having dinner.
4 was making a phone call.

**12.3**
1 The phone rang while I was taking a shower.
2 It began to rain while I was walking home.
3 We saw an accident while we were waiting for the bus.

**12.4**
1 fell . . . was painting
2 was reading . . . heard
3 Were you watching
4 was waiting . . . arrived
5 wasn't driving . . . happened
6 broke . . . was washing . . . slipped
7 took . . . wasn't looking
8 didn't go . . . was raining
9 were you doing
10 saw . . . was wearing

# Unit 13

Simple past is acceptable in 13.1, 13.2, 13.3, and 13.4.

**13.1**
1 Fred has gone to Brazil.
2 Jack and Jill have decided to get married.
3 Suzanne has had a baby.
4 Liz has given up smoking.
5 George has passed his driving test.

**13.2**
1 She has washed her hair.
2 He has lost weight.
3 It has run out of gas.
4 He has broken his leg.

**13.3**
1 Yes, I've just seen him.
2 Yes, she has just called.
3 No thanks, I've just put one out.

**13.4**
1 I've already called him.
2 I've already read it.
3 No, I've already paid (him).

**13.5**
1 been
2 gone
3 been

# Unit 14

**14.1**
1 Have you ever been to South America?
2 Have you read any English novels?
3 Have you lived in this town all your life?
4 How many times have you been in love?
5 What's the most beautiful country you have ever visited?
6 Have you ever spoken to a famous person?

**14.2**
1 movie I've ever seen.
2 longest book I've ever read.
3 interesting person I've ever met.

**14.3**
1 Is this the first time you've played tennis? Yes, I've never played tennis before.
2 Is this the first time you've ridden a horse? Yes, I've never ridden a horse before.
3 Is this the first time you've been to Canada? Yes, I've never been to Canada before.

**14.4**
1 hasn't rained
2 They haven't visited me since June.
3 I haven't played tennis for a long time.
4 I've never eaten caviar.
5 I haven't driven for six months.
6 I've never been to Puerto Rico. (For "been to" and "gone to" see Unit 13d.)
7 She hasn't written to me since last summer.

# Unit 15

**15.1**  1  Have you read a newspaper lately?
2  Have you seen Lisa in the past few days?
3  Have you played tennis lately?
4  Have you eaten anything today?
5  Have you seen any good movies lately?
6  Have you taken your vacation yet?

**15.2**  1  I haven't eaten there yet, but I'm going to eat there.
2  I haven't bought one yet, but I'm going to buy one.
3  He hasn't asked her yet, but he's going to ask her.

**15.3**  1  haven't eaten
2  hasn't snowed (much)
3  I haven't played (tennis) (much) so far
4  she hasn't worked hard so far
5  but I haven't watched television so far
6  haven't won

**15.4**  1  It's the second time you've been late this week.
2  It's the third time the car has broken down this month.
3  It's the fifth cup (of tea) she has had (*or* drunk) this morning.

# Unit 16

**16.1**  1  She has been working hard.
2  Bob and Bill have been fighting.
3  He has been lying in the sun.
4  She has been playing tennis.

**16.2**  1  Have you been crying?
2  Have you been waiting long?
3  What have you been doing?

**16.3**  1  He has been studying for three hours.
2  I've been learning Spanish since December.
3  She has been looking for a job for six months.
4  She has been working in Toronto since January 18th.
5  He has been smoking for five years.

**16.4**  1  How long has Sue been reading *War and Peace*?
2  How long has Mike been playing chess?
3  How long has Jim been selling washing machines?
4  How long has Linda been living on Main Street?

# Unit 17

**17.1**  1  She has been traveling around Europe for three months. She has visited six countries so far.
2  She has been playing tennis since she was 11. ("has played" is also possible – see Unit 18c.) She has won the national championship four times.
3  They have been making films since they left college. They have made ten films since they left college.

**17.2**  1  How long have you been waiting (for me)?
2  How many books have you written?
3  How long have you been writing books?
4  How many fish have you caught?

**17.3**  1  has broken
2  have been reading . . . haven't finished
3  haven't been waiting
4  have been cleaning . . . have cleaned
5  Have you been cooking
6  has appeared

# Unit 18

**18.1**   1  wrong – have been married
2  wrong – has been raining
3  right
4  wrong – have you always lived
5  wrong – has Ken had
6  wrong – have you known
7  right

**18.2**   1  How long has your sister been married?
2  How long has Carol been on vacation?
3  How long have you lived in Australia? / ... have you been living in Australia?
4  How long has it been snowing?
5  How long has Jack smoked? / ... has Jack been smoking?
6  How long have you known about her problem?
7  How long have Robert and Jill been looking for an apartment?
8  How long has Diana been teaching in Brazil? / ... has Diana taught in Brazil?

9  How long has Dennis been in love with Liz? / How long have they been in love?
10  How long has John had a car?

**18.3**   1  Jack has lived in Chicago since he was born.
2  Mary has been unemployed since April.
3  Ann has had a bad cold for the last few days.
4  I have wanted to go to the moon since I was a child.
5  My brother has been studying languages in college for two years.
6  Tim and Jane have been working in Peru since February.
7  My cousin has been in the army since he was 18.
8  They have been waiting for us for half an hour.

# Unit 19

**19.1**   1  How long has she been studying Italian? / When did she begin studying Italian?
2  How long have you known Tom? / When did you first meet Tom?
3  How long have they been married? / When did they get married?

**19.2**   1  since
2  for
3  for
4  Since
5  for
6  for

**19.3**   1  She has been sick for three days.
2  We got married five years ago.
3  He has had a beard for ten years.
4  She went to France three weeks ago.
5  He bought his new car in February.

**19.4**   1  No, it's been six months since I ate in a restaurant.
2  No, it's been years since it snowed here.
3  No, it's been a long time since I went swimming.

# Unit 20

**20.1**   1  wrong – Who wrote ...
2  wrong – Aristotle was ...
3  right
4  right
5  wrong – ... who developed ...
6  right

7  wrong – The U.S. bought ...
8  right
9  wrong – Did you visit ...
10  right
11  right
12  wrong – I didn't eat ... wasn't

**20.2**  1  I have been sick twice so far this year.
2  How many times were you sick last year?
3  I haven't drunk any coffee so far today.
4  He has been late three times this week.
5  How many games did the team win last season?
6  How many games has the team won so far this season?

**20.3**  1  worked
2  has lived
3  have been
4  was
5  has been
6  never met
7  have never met

# Unit 21

**21.1**  1  had gone
2  had closed
3  had died
4  had changed
5  had sold

**21.2**  1  I had never seen her before.
2  She had never been late before.
3  . . . she had never played (tennis) before.
4  He had never driven (a car) before.

**21.3**  1  He had just gone out.
2  The movie had already begun.
3  They had just finished their dinner.
4  She had already made plans to do something else.
5  I hadn't seen her for five years.

**21.4**  1  had gone
2  went
3  broke
4  had broken . . . stopped

# Unit 22

**22.1**  1  He had been studying hard all day.
2  Somebody had been smoking in the room.
3  She had been lying in the sun too long.
4  They had been playing football.
5  She had been dreaming.

**22.2**  1  The orchestra had been playing for about ten minutes when a man in the audience suddenly began shouting.
2  I had been waiting for 20 minutes when I realized that I had come to the wrong cafe.
3  They had been living in the south of France for six months when Mr. Jenkins died.

**22.3**  1  was looking
2  had been walking
3  were eating
4  had been eating
5  was waiting . . . had been waiting

# Unit 23

**23.1**
1 I don't have a ladder. (*or* I haven't got a ladder.)
2 We didn't have enough time.
3 He didn't have a map.
4 She doesn't have any money. (*or* She hasn't got any money.)
5 I didn't have any eggs.
6 I don't have my key. (*or* I haven't got my key.)
7 They didn't have a camera.
8 We didn't have an umbrella.

**23.2**
1 Do you have (*or* Have you got)
2 Did you have
3 Do you have (*or* Have you got)
4 Did you have
5 Did you have (*or* Have you got)
6 Did you have

**23.3**
2 had a party
3 have a nice day
4 had a baby
5 have a look
6 Did you have a good flight?
7 had a cigarette
8 have something to drink
9 Did you have a good time?

# Unit 24

**24.1**
1 used to cry
2 used to be
3 used to live
4 used to be
5 used to like
6 used to have / used to ride

**24.2** 1–4
– He used to go to bed early.
– He used to run three miles every morning.
– He never used to stay out late. / He didn't use to stay out late.
– He never used to spend a lot of money. / He didn't use to spend a lot of money.

**24.3**
1 he doesn't play tennis very much / very often / a lot.
2 she drinks coffee / it.
3 she is (fat).
4 he goes out a lot / very often. (*or* he often goes out.)

**24.4**
1 did he use to play the piano?
2 did he use to be rich?
3 did he use to go out often / very often / a lot?
4 did he use to dance?
5 did he use to have many friends?

# Unit 25

**25.1**
1 can / is able to
2 been able to
3 be able to
4 be able to

**25.2**
1 could play (tennis)
2 could run
3 could swim

**25.3**
1 were able to find it.
2 was able to win (it).
3 was able to escape.

**25.4**
1 couldn't / wasn't able to
2 was able to
3 could / was able to
4 was able to
5 could / was able to
6 were able to

# Unit 26

**26.1**  1  We could have fish.
2  We could go (and see him) on Friday.
3  You could give her a book (for her birthday).

**26.2**  1  We could have gone to the concert, but we decided not to.
2  He could have taken the exam, but he decided not to.
3  I could have bought a new car, but I decided not to.

**26.3**  1  But he could have helped us.
2  But he could help us.

3  But they could lend us some (money).
4  But she could have had something to eat.

**26.4**  1  He couldn't have come (to a party on Friday night) because he was sick.
2  He could have played tennis on Monday afternoon.
3  He couldn't have translated it because he doesn't know any Spanish.
4  He could have lent Jack $20.
5  He couldn't have fixed her washing machine because he doesn't know anything about machines.

# Unit 27

**27.1**  1  they must be married.
2  he can't be serious.
3  they must have been in a hurry.
4  she must know a lot of people.
5  he must have known about it / the plan.
6  they can't have much (money).
7  she can't have been driving carefully.
8  they must be waiting for somebody.

Short answers are also possible in this exercise:
1  they must be.
2  he can't be.
3  they must have been.
4  she must.
5  he must have.
6  they can't have.
7  she can't have been.
8  they must be.

**27.2**  1  must have
2  can't be
3  must be
4  must read / must have read
5  must be going

**27.3**  1  It must have been very expensive.
2  He must have gone away.
3  You must have left it on the bus.
4  The exam can't have been very difficult.
5  She must have listened / must have been listening to our conversation.
6  He can't have understood what I said.
7  I must have forgotten to turn it off.
8  The driver can't have seen the red light.

# Unit 28

**28.1**  1  I'm not sure. They may/might be married.
2  I'm not sure. She may/might want to go.
3  I'm not sure. He may/might be telling the truth.
4  I'm not sure. He may/might have a car.
5  I'm not sure. She may/might have been sick.
6  I'm not sure. She may/might have told somebody.

7  I'm not sure. They may/might have been listening.
8  I'm not sure. She may/might not want to go.
9  I'm not sure. He may/might not be telling the truth.
10  I'm not sure. They may/might not be ready.

**28.2**  1  a) She may be going to the theater.
           b) She could be going to a party.
        2  a) He may have gone to bed early.
           b) He might not have heard the bell.
        3  a) Someone may have dropped a
              cigarette.
           b) It could have been a short circuit.

        4  a) She might have been going to work.
           b) She may have been going shopping.
        5  a) He might have had to go somewhere
              else.
           b) He may not have known about it.

# Unit 29

**29.1**  1  I may/might buy a Toyota.
        2  I may/might go skiing.
        3  I may/might hang it in the dining room.
        4  he may/might come tomorrow evening.
        5  she may/might go to a business college.

**29.2**  1  He may be late.
        2  She might not be able to find it / our
           house.
        3  There might be a rainstorm tonight.

        4  He may not pass it / the exam.
        5  They might be waiting for us when we
           arrive.
        6  It may snow later.

**29.3**  1  We may/might as well have another
           cup.
        2  I may/might as well go (to the concert).
        3  We may/might as well begin/start.

# Unit 30

**30.1**  1  Could I borrow your camera?
        2  Can I give/offer you a lift?
        3  Could you tell me how to get to the
           airport? / Could you tell me the way to
           the airport?
        4  Do you think I could come and see it /
           the apartment today?
        5  May I smoke?
        6  Do you think I could leave (work)
           early?
        7  Would you like to come and stay (with
           me) for the weekend?
        8  Do you think you could turn it / the
           music down?

**30.2**  1  Could/Can you show me how to change
           the film? / Do you think you could
           show me how . . . ?
        2  Could/May/Can I look at your
           newspaper? / Do you think I could have
           a look . . . ?
        3  Could/Can you give me a light? /
           Could/May/Can I have a light?
        4  Would you like to come to a/the
           concert tonight?
        5  Could/May/Can I have three airmail
           stamps?
        6  Would you like a seat? / Would you
           like to sit down? / Can I offer you a
           seat?
        7  Would you like to come to a party next
           Saturday?

# Unit 31

**31.1**  1  must / have to ("must" is better – the
           speaker is giving a personal opinion)
        2  have to / must ("have to" is better – the
           speaker is just giving a fact)
        3  had to
        4  had to (*present perfect*)
        5  have to / must ("have to" is better – the
           speaker is just giving a fact)

        6  had to
        7  have to
        8  had to
        9  must / have to ("must" is better – the
           speaker is giving a personal opinion)

**31.2**
1 . . . does she have to leave?
2 . . . did you have to answer?
3 . . . did he have to pay?
4 . . . do you have to get up early tomorrow?

**31.3**
1 . . . didn't have to pay (to get into the concert).
2 . . . he doesn't have to shave.
3 . . . I didn't have to get up early.
4 . . . I don't have to work.

**31.4**
1 don't have to
2 mustn't
3 mustn't
4 doesn't have to
5 don't have to

# Unit 32

In all of the exercises in Unit 32 "ought to / ought not to" is possible instead of "should/shouldn't."

**32.1**
1 You should go to the dentist.
2 You shouldn't ride your bicycle at night without lights.
3 You should learn a few words of Greek before you go.

**32.2**
1 I think all drivers should wear seat belts.
2 I don't think Jill and Sam should get married.
3 I think you should stay home tonight.

**32.3**
1 She should be wearing a coat. / She should wear a coat. / She should have put a coat on.
2 We should have brought something to eat.
3 You should have come to see me (when you were in Paris).
4 It / The store should be open.
5 She shouldn't have stopped (so) suddenly (without warning). / She should have given warning that she was going to stop.
6 They should be in bed. They shouldn't be watching television.
7 Tom shouldn't have been driving on the wrong side of the road.

# Unit 33

**33.1**
1 She insisted that I stay a little longer.
2 I suggested that she visit the museum after lunch.
3 The doctor recommended that I see a specialist.
4 The landlord demanded that the tenant pay the rent by Friday at the latest.
5 Jack suggested that I go away for a few days.
6 Alice proposed that we have dinner early.

**33.2**
1 spend
2 leave
3 be
4 sell
5 apologize
6 be
7 wear
8 be

**33.3**
2 Bill suggested that he eat more fruit and vegetables.
3 Sandra suggested that he walk to work in the morning.
4 Linda suggested that he try jogging.

# Unit 34

**34.1**
1 would take
2 refused
3 closed
4 wouldn't get
5 didn't come
6 took
7 would be
8 walked
9 didn't go
10 would understand

**34.2**
1 What would you do if a millionaire asked you to marry him/her?
2 What would you do if you lost your passport in a foreign country?
3 What would you do if somebody threw an egg at you?
4 What would you do if your car was stolen?
5 What would you do if somebody parked a car on your foot?

**34.3**
1 If he took the exam, he would fail it.
2 If I invited Bill to the party, I would have to invite Linda too.
3 If I went to bed now, I wouldn't sleep.
4 If she applied for the job, she wouldn't get it.

# Unit 35

**35.1**
1 would give
2 had
3 didn't go
4 were
5 could
6 wouldn't marry
7 weren't

**35.2**
1 But if he spoke (more) clearly, people would understand him.
2 But if that book weren't so expensive, I would buy it.
3 But if she could walk without help, she would go out more often.
4 But if he got some/more exercise, he wouldn't be (so) fat.
5 But if it weren't raining, we could (*or* would be able to) have lunch outside.
6 But if I didn't have to work, I could (*or* would be able to) meet you tomorrow evening.

**35.3**
1 I wish I could give up smoking.
2 I wish I had a cigarette / some cigarettes.
3 I wish George were here.
4 I wish it weren't so cold. (*or* I wish it were warm.)
5 I wish I didn't live in New York City.
6 I wish Tina could come to the party.
7 I wish I didn't have to work tomorrow. (*or* I wish I could stay in bed tomorrow.)
8 I wish I knew something about cars.
9 I wish I were lying on a beautiful sunny beach.

# Unit 36

**36.1**  1  had missed
         2  would have forgotten
         3  hadn't recommended
         4  had had (*or* if I'd had)

**36.2**  1  If the driver in front hadn't stopped (so) suddenly, the accident wouldn't have happened.
         2  If I had known George wanted (*or* had wanted) to get up early, I would have woken him.
         3  If Jim hadn't lent me the money, I wouldn't have been able to buy the car.
         4  If she hadn't been wearing (*or* hadn't worn) a seat belt, she would have been injured in the crash.

         5  If you'd had (= had had) breakfast, you wouldn't be hungry now.
         6  If she'd had (= had had) enough money on her, she would have bought the coat.

**36.3**  1  I wish I hadn't painted the door red. / I wish I had painted it another color.
         2  I wish I had brought my camera. / I wish I had my camera with me.
         3  I wish I had seen him. / I wish I had been here when he came.
         4  I wish the hotel had been better. / I wish we had stayed at another (*or* a nicer) hotel.

# Unit 37

**37.1**  1  I wish Tim would come. / I wish Tim would hurry (up).
         2  I wish that baby would stop crying / be quiet.
         3  I wish somebody would give me a job.
         4  I wish you would buy some new clothes.

**37.2**  1  I wish the man in the apartment next door wouldn't play the piano in the middle of the night.
         2  I wish people wouldn't drop litter in the street.

         3  I wish you wouldn't always leave the door open.

**37.3**  1  He promised (me) he would write to me.
         2  She promised (me) she wouldn't tell Tom what I said.
         3  They promised (me) they would come.

**37.4**  1  would shake
         2  would be
         3  would always take

# Unit 38

**38.1**    1  He's going to take some chocolate in case he gets hungry.
     2–5  He's going to take an umbrella in case it rains.
            He's going to take a towel in case he wants to go swimming.
            He's going to take a map in case he gets lost.
            He's going to take some lemonade in case he gets thirsty.

**38.2**    1  I gave him my address in case he came to Los Angeles one day.

         2  I said goodbye in case I didn't see her again.
         3  She called her parents in case they were worried about her.
         4  I wrote down the name of the street in case I forgot it.
         5  I wrote them a second letter in case they hadn't received the first one.

**38.3**  1  If        5  in case
         2  in case   6  if
         3  in case   7  in case
         4  if

# Unit 39

**39.1**  1  You won't know what to do unless you listen carefully.
2  We'll miss the train unless we hurry.
3  He won't be able to understand you unless you speak very slowly.
4  I'll look for another job unless I get a raise.
5  I won't forgive her unless she apologizes to me.

**39.2**  1  I'm not going to the party unless you go too.

2  You're not allowed into the club unless you're a member.
3  The dog won't attack you unless you move.
4  She won't speak to you unless you ask her a question.

**39.3**
| | | | |
|---|---|---|---|
| 1 | unless | 5 | providing |
| 2 | provided | 6 | unless |
| 3 | as long as | 7 | unless |
| 4 | unless | | |

# Unit 40

**40.1**
1  be made
2  be knocked
3  be checked
4  be woken
5  be translated
6  be arrested
7  be found
8  be spent
9  be carried
10  be driven

**40.2**
1  might have been invited
2  would have been seen
3  must have been fixed.
4  shouldn't have been thrown away.

**40.3**
1  Complaints should be sent to the main office.
2  The meeting had to be postponed because of illness.
3  Your car might have been stolen if you had left the keys in it.
4  The fire could have been caused by a short circuit.
5  Next year's convention is going to be held in San Francisco.
6  The soccer match shouldn't have been played in such bad weather.

# Unit 41

**41.1**
1  Service is included in the bill.
2  This road isn't used very often.
3  All flights were canceled because of fog.
4  I was accused of stealing the money.
5  A new shopping center is being built downtown.
6  I didn't realize that our conversation was being recorded.
7  The date of the meeting has been changed.
8  Brian told me that he had been attacked and robbed in the street.

**41.2**
1  Every week it is watched by millions of people.
2  Are most of them exported?
3  About 20 people were arrested.
4  When was it abolished?
5  But nobody was injured so it wasn't needed.
6  Was anything taken?
7  It is being redecorated.
8  It was being tuned up at the garage.
9  It has been stolen!
10  They haven't been seen since then.
11  Has it been painted since I was last here?
12  It had been blown down in the storm.

# Unit 42

**42.1**
1   Jim isn't paid very much.
2   You will be asked a lot of questions at the interview.
3   I wasn't told that Liz was sick.
4   He was given a present by his colleagues when he retired.
5   You will be sent your exam results as soon as they are ready.
6   I wasn't asked my name.
7   I think Tom should have been offered the job.

**42.2**
2   Shakespeare was born in 1564.
3   Leonardo da Vinci was born in 1452.
4   Charlie Chaplin was born in 1889.
5   Beethoven was born in 1770.
6   I was born in . . .

**42.3**
1   being invited        4   being paid
2   being attacked       5   being used
3   being asked          6   being given

**42.4**
1   got stung            4   get used
2   get broken           5   got stolen
3   get damaged

# Unit 43

**43.1**
1   Many people are said to be homeless because of the flood.
2   The Governor is known to be in favor of the new law.
3   The President is expected to lose the election.
4   The thieves are believed to have gotten in through the kitchen window.
5   She is alleged to have driven through the town at 90 miles an hour.
6   Two people are reported to have been seriously injured in the accident.
7   Three men are said to have been arrested after the explosion.

**43.2**
1   Arthur is supposed to be very rich.
2   He is supposed to have 22 children.
3   He is supposed to sleep on a bed of nails.
4   He is supposed to have inherited a lot of money.
5   He is supposed to write poetry.

**43.3**
1   are supposed to be
2   is supposed to study
3   aren't supposed to have
4   was supposed to call
5   weren't supposed to come

# Unit 44

**44.1**
1   I had it cut.
2   they had it painted.
3   he had it cut down.
4   she had it repaired.

**44.2**
1   have (*or* get) it cut.
2   do you have (*or* get) your car tuned up?
3   have (*or* get) a new engine put in.
4   Do you have (*or* get) your newspaper delivered
5   am having a swimming pool built.
6   haven't had (*or* gotten) the film developed yet.
7   had his portrait painted

**44.3**
1   He is going to have his eyes tested. (*or* He is going to have an eye exam.)
2   She is having her hair cut.
3   She has had her watch repaired.

**44.4**
1   He had his wallet stolen from his pocket.
2   He had his hat blown off by the wind.
3   She had her passport taken from her at the police station.

# Unit 45

**45.1**
2 Helen said that her father was in the hospital.
3 She said (that) Sue and Jim were getting married next month.
4 She said (that) she hadn't seen Bill for a while.
5 She said (that) she had been playing tennis a lot lately.
6 She said (that) Barbara had had a baby.
7 She said (that) she didn't know what Fred was doing.
8 She said (that) she hardly ever went out these days.
9 She said (that) she worked 14 hours a day.
10 She said (that) she would tell Jim she had seen me. / . . . she saw me.
11 She said (that) I could come and stay with her if I was ever in Toronto.
12 She said (that) Tom had had an accident last week but he hadn't been injured. / . . . Tom had an accident last week but he wasn't injured.
13 She said (that) she had seen Jack at a party a few months ago and he had seemed fine. / . . . she saw Jack . . . and he seemed fine.

**45.2**
1 I thought you said she wasn't coming to the party.
2 I thought you said (that) he hadn't passed his exam. / . . . he didn't pass his exam.
3 I thought you said (that) Ann didn't like Bill.
4 I thought you said (that) you hadn't got many friends. / . . . you didn't have many friends.
5 I thought you said (that) they weren't going to get married.
6 I thought you said (that) he didn't work very hard.
7 I thought you said (that) you didn't want to be rich and famous.
8 I thought you said (that) you wouldn't be here next week.
9 I thought you said (that) you couldn't afford a vacation this year.

---

# Unit 46

**46.1**
1 You said (that) you were hungry.
2 Tom told me (that) you had gone away.
3 You said (that) you didn't smoke.
4 You said (that) you wouldn't be late. / You told me (that) you . . .
5 You said (that) you couldn't come to the party tonight. / You told me (that) you . . .
6 You said (that) you were working tomorrow evening. / You told me (that) you . . .

**46.2**
| | | | |
|---|---|---|---|
| 1 | told | 5 | told |
| 2 | said | 6 | said |
| 3 | said | 7 | talked |
| 4 | told | 8 | told |

**46.3**
1 The doctor said to eat more fruit and vegetables.
2 He told me to read the instructions before I used the machine.
3 She told us to shut the door but not to lock it.
4 He asked me to speak more slowly because he couldn't understand.
5 I told her not to come before 6:00.

## Unit 47

**47.1**  1  Where do Ed and Liz live?
2  How long have they been married?
3  Do they go out very often?
4  What does Liz do for a living?
5  Does she like being a teacher?
6  What does Ed do for a living?
7  Does he enjoy his job?
8  Did he arrest anyone yesterday?
9  Do they have a car? / Have they got a car?
10  When did they buy it?
11  Are they going on vacation next summer? / Are they going to go on vacation next summer?
12  Where are they going? / Where are they going to go?

**47.2**  1  What happened?
2  Who lives in that house?
3  Who gave you this/that key?
4  What did Henry give you?
5  Who does Tom meet every day?
6  What did you fall over?
7  What fell on the floor?
8  What does this word mean?

**47.3**  1  Don't you like him?
2  Don't you have any? / Haven't you got any?
3  Isn't it good?

**47.4**  1  Why don't you like George?
2  Why wasn't Jim at work today?
3  Why aren't you ready yet?
4  Why doesn't Sue eat fruit?
5  Why can't Maria come to the meeting?

## Unit 48

**48.1**  1  Could you tell me where the post office is?
2  Do you know what this word means?
3  I wonder what time it is.
4  Can't you remember where you parked your car?
5  I don't know whether (*or* if) Ann is coming to the meeting.
6  Do you have any idea where Jack lives?
7  Do you know what time he left?
8  Could you tell me where I can change some money?
9  I want to know what qualifications I need.
10  I don't know why Mary didn't come to the party.
11  Do you know how much it costs to park here?

**48.2**  1  where she has gone
2  when she will be back
3  whether (*or* if) she went out alone

**48.3**  2  He asked me how long I had been back.
3  He asked (me) what I was doing now.
4  He asked (me) where I was living.
5  He asked (me) whether (*or* if) I was glad to be back.
6  He asked (me) whether (*or* if) I was going away again.
7  He asked (me) why I had come back. / . . . why I came back.
8  He asked (me) whether (*or* if) I still smoked.
9  He asked (me) whether (*or* if) I could come to dinner on Friday.

## Unit 49

**49.1**  1  Do you? I don't.
2  Can't you? I can.
3  Do you? I don't.
4  Didn't you? I did.
5  Would you? I wouldn't.
6  Don't you? I do.
7  Aren't you? I am.
8  Haven't you? I have.
9  Did you? I didn't.

**49.2**   1   So do I.              6   So was I.          **49.3**   1   I hope so.
           2   Neither do I.         7   So should I.                  2   I guess so.
           3   Neither could I.      8   So did I.                     3   I don't think so.
           4   So would I.           9   Neither did I.                4   I'm afraid not.
           5   Neither have I.                                         5   I'm afraid so.
                                                                       6   I guess so.
           "Nor" is possible instead of "neither" in this             7   I hope not.
           exercise.                                                  8   I think so.

## Unit 50

**50.1**   1   isn't she              **50.2**   1   It's a beautiful day, isn't it?
           2   were you                          2   The movie was great, wasn't it?
           3   does she                          3   You've had your hair cut, haven't you?
           4   didn't he                             / You've had a haircut, haven't you? *or*
           5   don't you                             You had your hair cut, didn't you? /
           6   can't you                             You had a haircut, didn't you?
           7   will he                           4   It doesn't look very good, does it?
           8   couldn't he                       5   Bill works very hard, doesn't he?
           9   aren't there
          10   shall we              **50.3**   1   Jack, you couldn't get me some stamps,
          11   is it                                could you?
          12   aren't I                          2   Alan, you don't know where Ann is, do
          13   would you                             you? / Alan, you haven't seen Ann,
          14   should I                              have you?
          15   didn't they                       3   Tom, you don't have any paper, do
          16   had he ("He'd" = He had)              you? / Tom, you couldn't lend (*or* give)
                                                     me some paper, could you?
                                                 4   Ann, you couldn't give me a lift, could
                                                     you?
                                                 5   Liz, you haven't seen my purse, have
                                                     you? / Liz, you don't know where my
                                                     purse is, do you?

## Unit 51

**51.1**   1   making                **51.2**   1   I wouldn't mind going out this evening.
           2   writing                           2   Do you regret not taking the job?
           3   meeting                               (*or* . . . that you didn't take . . . )
           4   taking                            3   Why don't you put off going away until
           5   splashing                             tomorrow?
           6   trying                            4   It's better to avoid traveling during the
           7   washing                               rush hour.
           8   eating                            5   Would you mind turning the radio
           9   stealing . . . driving                down, please?
          10   looking                           6   The driver of the car admitted not
          11   going                                 having a license. (*or* . . . that he didn't
          12   being run (*passive*)                 have a license.)
                                                 7   Sue suggested having fish for dinner.
                                                     (*or* . . . suggested that we have fish /
                                                     suggested that we should have fish . . . )

**51.3** If possible check your sentences with someone who speaks English. Here are some sample answers:

1 On weekends I enjoy sitting in the garden (if it's warm).
2 I dislike going out to eat in fancy restaurants.

3 I often regret not traveling more when I was younger.
4 Learning English involves speaking as much as you can.
5 I think people should stop watching television so much.

# Unit 52

**52.1**
1 to lend / to give
2 to buy / to rent / to get
3 to shut / to close / to lock
4 to get ("arrive" is not possible because we say "arrive *at* the airport")
5 (how) to fly / to pilot (*not* "to drive")
6 to hear / to understand / to see
7 to be / to come / to arrive
8 to call / to telephone / to phone
9 to take
10 (to) talk / (to) speak / (to) laugh / (to) play (After "dare" you can use the infinitive with or without "to" – see section c.)
11 to come / to go
12 to buy / to get / to pick up

**52.2**
1 He seems to be worried about something.
2 She appears to like Jack.
3 He appears to be looking for something.
4 It seems to have broken down.
5 They appear to have gone out.

**52.3**
1 what to cook
2 how to use
3 what to do
4 how to ride
5 what to say ("what to do" is also possible)

**52.4** If possible check your answers with someone who speaks English. Here are some sample answers:

1 Not many people can afford to buy a Rolls Royce.
2 I would like to learn (how) to ride a horse.
3 One day I hope to have enough money to travel around the world.
4 I wouldn't dare (to) wear clothes like that. I would look stupid.
5 Sometimes I tend to be a bit lazy.
6 I intend to get my work done on time.

# Unit 53

**53.1**
1 They wanted Tom to stay with them.
2 I don't want anyone to know.
3 Do you want Navy to win?
4 I wanted it to be a surprise.

**53.2**
1 Jack reminded me to mail the letter.
2 She advised me to tell the police about the accident.
3 I warned you not to tell him anything.
4 I didn't expect it to rain. (*or* . . . expect that it would rain.)
5 Tom invited Ann to have dinner with him. (*or* Tom invited Ann to dinner with him.)
6 Jane persuaded me to play tennis.

7 The sudden noise made me jump.
8 Having a car enables you to travel around more easily.
9 She wouldn't let me read the letter.

**53.3**
1 smoke
2 to meet
3 to go
4 eating
5 cry
6 to study
7 to go (= we *were* allowed to go – *passive*)
8 clean (*or* to clean)

# Unit 54

**54.1**
1 I like wearing a hat. / I like to wear hats (*or* a hat).
2 She enjoys watching television.
3 I don't like staying up late. / I don't like to stay up late.
4 He likes taking pictures. / He likes to take pictures.
5 I hate working in the evenings. / I hate to work in the evenings.

**54.2**
1 traveling
2 cooking / to cook . . . cleaning / to clean
3 to live
4 driving / to drive
5 getting / to get
6 listening
7 to come
8 to learn

**54.3** If possible check your sentences with someone who speaks English. Here are some sample answers:
1 I don't like playing cards very much. (*or* I don't like to play . . . )
2 I enjoy learning languages.
3 I don't mind visiting museums.
4 I love lying on the beach in the sun. (*or* I love to lie . . . )
5 I hate shopping. (*or* I hate to shop.)

**54.4**
1 I would love to have met Ann.
2 I would hate to have lost my watch.
3 I wouldn't like to have been alone.
4 I would prefer to have gone by train.
5 I would like to have seen the movie.

In this exercise it is also possible to use another structure:
1 I would have loved to meet Ann.
2 I would have hated to lose my watch.
3 I wouldn't have liked to be alone.
4 I would have preferred to go by train.
5 I would have liked to see the movie.

# Unit 55

**55.1**
2 He can remember going to Los Angeles when he was eight.
3 He can't remember falling into the lake.
4 He can remember crying on his first day of school.
5 He can't remember saying he wanted to be a doctor. (*or* He can't remember wanting to be a doctor.)
6 He can't remember being bitten by a dog.

**55.2**
1 Have you tried changing the batteries?
2 Have you tried phoning him at work?
3 Have you tried taking sleeping pills? (*or* Have you tried sleeping pills?)
4 Have you tried moving the antenna?

**55.3**
1 lending
2 to put
3 to give
4 leaving
5 to laugh (*or* laughing)
6 asking
7 to reach
8 to call
9 to make (*or* making)

# Unit 56

**56.1**
1 Before going to bed, Liz had a hot drink. (*or* Before she went . . . )
2 Soon after taking off, the plane crashed. (*or* Soon after it took . . . / Soon after it had taken . . . )
3 Instead of eating at home, we went to a restaurant.
4 You put people's lives in danger by driving dangerously.
5 In spite of hurting his leg, he managed to win the race.
6 Bill is very good at cooking.
7 I have no intention of lending her any money.
8 By exercising more, George lost 10 pounds.
9 She was angry with me for being late.
10 Jane prefers doing nothing to working.

**56.2**
1 He translated the article without using a dictionary.
2 Don't cross the street without looking right and left (first).
3 She got married without anybody knowing about it.

**56.3**
1 I'm looking forward to seeing him/her again. (*or* I'm looking forward to him/his*/her coming.)
2 I'm not looking forward to going to the dentist.
3 She is looking forward to graduating.

*You can say "I'm looking forward to *his* . . . ing . . . " or "I'm looking forward to *him* . . . ing . . . ."

# Unit 57

**57.1**
1 in finding
2 of/about looking
3 of his staying
4 from coming
5 to having
6 like studying
7 for interrupting
8 of breaking
9 of/about getting
10 of living
11 from going
12 of committing
13 for being
14 against buying (*or* decided not to buy)

**57.2**
1 Tom insisted on driving Ann to the airport.
2 Jim congratulated me on passing my exams.
3 Mrs. Richmond thanked Sue for visiting her.
4 I warned Jack against staying at the hotel near the airport. (You can also say "I warned Jack not to stay . . . " – see Unit 53b.)
5 Margaret apologized (to me) for not calling (me) earlier.
6 The teacher accused the boy of not paying attention to what he/she (had) said.

**57.3** If possible check your answers with someone who speaks English. Here are some sample answers:
1 This evening I feel like going to the movies.
2 I'm looking forward to seeing Ann next week.
3 I'm thinking of buying a new camera.
4 I would never dream of leaving without saying goodbye.

# Unit 58

**58.1**
1. It's no use trying to escape.
2. It's a waste of money smoking.
3. It's no use asking Tom to help you.
4. It's not worth hurrying.
5. There's no point in studying if you're feeling tired.
6. It's a waste of time reading newspapers.
7. It's not worth getting angry.
8. There's no point in working if you don't need the money.

**58.2**
1. The museum is worth visiting.
2. Those shoes aren't worth repairing.
3. These old clothes aren't worth keeping.
4. The plan is worth considering.

**58.3**
1. Tom has difficulty/trouble meeting people.
2. She had no difficulty/trouble finding a job.
3. You won't have any difficulty/trouble getting a ticket for the concert.
4. I have difficulty/trouble understanding him when he speaks quickly.

**58.4**
2. go skiing
3. went swimming
4. goes riding
5. go shopping

# Unit 59

**59.1**
1. a) At first he wasn't used to having dinner at 6:00.
   b) But after some time he got used to having dinner at 6:00.
   c) He is used to having dinner at 6:00.
2. a) At first she wasn't used to working nights.
   b) But after a while she got used to working nights.
   c) She is used to working nights.

**59.2**
1. He is used to sleeping on the floor.
2. She had to get used to living in a smaller house.

3. He wasn't used to the heat. (There is no verb after "used to" in this example.)
4. He is used to having no money.
5. (*sample answer*) She'll have to get used to driving on the right side of the road.

**59.3**
1. go
2. wearing
3. be
4. being
5. eating
6. like
7. running
8. go

# Unit 60

**60.1**
1. I have to go to the bank to change some money.
2. She knocked on my door to wake me up.
3. I'm saving money to go to Europe.
4. Ron is going into the hospital to have an operation. (*or* Ron is going into the hospital for an operation.)
5. I'm wearing two sweaters to keep warm.
6. I went to the police station to report that my car had been stolen.

**60.2**
1. to celebrate
2. to read / to buy
3. to sleep
4. to wear
5. to climb / to go up
6. to discuss / to consider / to talk about / to solve / to study / to examine
7. to put / to pack / to keep / to store
8. to hang / to put
9. to buy / to get
10. to talk / to speak
11. to go / to travel

**60.3**  1  We wore warm clothes so that we wouldn't get cold.
2  I spoke very slowly so that the man would understand what I said. / . . . could understand what I said.
3  I whispered so that no one would hear our conversation. / . . . could hear . . . / . . . would be able to hear . . .
4  Please arrive early so that we can start the meeting on time. / . . . so that we will be able to start . . .
5  She locked the door so that she wouldn't be disturbed.
6  I slowed down so that the car behind could pass me. / . . . would be able to pass me.

## Unit 61

**61.1**  1  I prefer San Francisco to Los Angeles.
2  I prefer calling people to writing letters.
3  I prefer going to the movies to watching movies on TV.
4  I prefer to call people rather than write letters.
5  I prefer to go to the movies rather than watch movies on TV.

**61.2**  1  I'd rather go for a swim.
2  I'd rather read a book.
3  I'd rather wait for a few minutes.
4  I'd rather eat at home.
5  I'd rather think about it for a while.

6  I'd rather go for a swim than play tennis.
7  I'd rather read a book than watch television.
8  I'd rather wait for a few minutes than leave now.
9  I'd rather eat at home than go to a restaurant.
10  I'd rather think about it for a while than decide now.

**61.3**  1  I'd rather you called him.
2  I'd rather you did them.
3  I'd rather you went.
4  I'd rather you told her.

## Unit 62

**62.1**  1  You'd better sit down.
2  We'd better take a taxi.
3  You'd better not play the piano (now / so late).
4  We'd better make a reservation.
5  You'd better put a Band-Aid on it.
6  I'd better have the oil changed (before I go on vacation).
7  We'd better not swim in that river.

**62.2**  1  It's time I took a vacation.
2  It's time Tom wrote to his parents.
3  It's time this room was redecorated.
4  It's time Ann was here. / . . . time Ann came. / . . . time Ann arrived.
5  It's time the plane took off.
6  It's time the government stopped spending money on weapons and concentrated on raising the standard of living.
7  It's time I got dinner ready.
8  It's time I went to the dentist.

## Unit 63

**63.1**  1  I've never seen her smoke/smoking.
2  I saw him take the money.
3  Yes, I heard him lock the door.
4  I didn't hear it ring.

5  I've heard her play/playing the piano.
6  Yes, I saw him trip over the dog.
7  I didn't see her fall into the river.

**63.2**
2 We saw Sue playing tennis.
3 We saw Tom eating in that restaurant.
4 We heard Bill playing the guitar.
5 We smelled dinner burning.
6 We saw Dave talking to Chuck.

**63.3**
3 tell
4 crying
5 collide
6 run ... open ... climb
7 explode
8 crawling
9 slam
10 sitting

# Unit 64

**64.1**
1 Jill was lying on the bed crying.
2 I got home feeling very tired.
3 The old man was walking along the street talking to himself.
4 Ann fell asleep watching television.
5 The man slipped getting off the bus.
6 The girl was run over crossing the street.
7 The fire fighter was overcome by smoke trying to put out the fire.

**64.2**
1 Having bought our tickets, we went into the theater.
2 Having had dinner, they continued on their trip.
3 Having done all her shopping, Sue went for a cup of coffee.

**64.3**
1 Thinking they might be hungry, I offered them something to eat.
2 Being a foreigner, she needs a visa to stay in this country.
3 Not knowing his address, I couldn't contact him.
4 Not being able to understand English, the man didn't know what I said.
5 Having traveled a lot, she knows a lot about other countries.
6 Having spent nearly all our money, we couldn't afford to stay in a hotel.

# Unit 65

**65.1**
1 hair
2 very good weather
3 luggage
4 a (= a newspaper)
5 some
6 job
7 doesn't
8 trip
9 furniture
10 complete chaos
11 some
12 experience

**65.2**
1 experience / any experience / much experience / enough experience
2 information
3 hair
4 progress / some progress / a lot of progress

5 any paper / some paper / a piece of paper
6 permission (*not* the permission)
7 work / some work (*not* a work)
8 advice / some advice / his advice

**65.3**
1 I'd like some information (*or* advice) about places to see in the town.
2 What beautiful weather! / What a beautiful day!
3 Can you give me some advice about which exams to take? / ... about which exams I should take?
4 What time is the news on (television)?
5 What a beautiful view! / What beautiful scenery!

## Unit 66

**66.1**
1  It's a vegetable.
2  It's a bird.
3  It's a flower. / It's a weed.
4  It's a (very) tall building.
5  They are planets.
6  They are rivers.
7  He was an artist / a painter / a sculptor.
8  He was a playwright / a writer / a poet.
9  He was a scientist / a physicist.
10  She was a movie star / an actress.
11  They were American presidents.
12  They were singers/musicians.

**66.2**
1  She is a typist / a secretary / a receptionist.
2  He is a travel agent.
3  She is a nurse.
4  She is a math teacher.
5  She is a movie director.
6  He is an interpreter.

**66.3**
| | | | |
|---|---|---|---|
| 1 | a | 9 | Some |
| 2 | an | 10 | – . . . a (fast runner) |
| 3 | – | 11 | a . . . some |
| 4 | – | 12 | some |
| 5 | some *or* – | 13 | a . . . – |
| 6 | – | 14 | some |
| 7 | a | 15 | – |
| 8 | – | 16 | a |

## Unit 67

**67.1**
1  This morning I bought *a* newspaper and *a* magazine. *The* newspaper is in my bag, but I don't know where *the* magazine is.
2  My parents have *a* cat and *a* dog. *The* dog never bites *the* cat, but *the* cat often scratches *the* dog.
3  I saw *an* accident this morning. *A* car crashed into *a* wall. *The* driver of *the* car was not hurt, but *the* car was badly damaged.
4  When you turn onto Pine Street Drive, you will see three houses: *a* red one, *a* blue one, and *a* white one. I live in *the* white one.
5  We live in *an* old house in *the* middle of town. There is *a* garden behind the house. *The* roof of *the* house is in bad condition.

**67.2**
| | | | |
|---|---|---|---|
| 1 | an | 8 | the |
| 2 | the | 9 | a |
| 3 | a . . . the | 10 | The |
| 4 | the | 11 | a . . . the |
| 5 | a . . . The | 12 | the |
| 6 | the . . . the | 13 | a . . . a |
| 7 | a | 14 | The |

**67.3**
| | | | |
|---|---|---|---|
| 1 | the floor | 6 | the police |
| 2 | the fire department | 7 | the doctor |
| 3 | the post office | 8 | the bank |
| 4 | the dentist | 9 | the airport |
| 5 | the station | 10 | the hospital |

## Unit 68

**68.1**
1  the biggest hotel
2  the richest man
3  the worst accident
4  the cheapest restaurant
5  the hottest (day)

**68.2**
1  the
2  The . . . the
3  . . . *the* first country to send a man into *space*
4  *on television* or in *a* movie theater

5 *After lunch* ... by *the* sea.
6 a
7 the
8 a ... the
9 a ... The
10 the ... a
11 a ... The ... the
12 *to dinner*
13 the ... the
14 the ... the ... a

15 *at sea*
16 the
17 the (= the television set)

**68.3** 2 he listened to *the* radio.
3 he went for a walk in *the* country.
4 he *had lunch.*
5 he went to *the* movies.
6 he *had dinner.*
7 From 8:00 until (*or* to) 10:00 he *watched television.*

# Unit 69

**69.1** If possible check your answers with someone who speaks English. Here are some sample answers:
1 the pine
2 the eagle
3 the Toyota
4 the flute

**69.2** 1 Jack plays *the* guitar very badly.
2 Jill plays *the* violin in an orchestra.
3 I'd like to learn to play *the* piano.
4 Do you play *the* guitar? / Can you play *the* guitar?

**69.3** 1 *The* cheetah ...
2 *The* whale ...
3 *The* ostrich ...

**69.4** 1 the dead ... The injured
2 the rich ... the poor

3 the unemployed
4 the sick

**69.5** 1 the British
2 the Irish
3 the Greeks
4 the Koreans
5 the Spanish (*or* the Spaniards)
6 the French
7 the Japanese
8 the Germans
9 the Chinese
10 the Canadians
11 the Swiss
12 the Americans
13 the Dutch
14 ???

# Unit 70

**70.1** If possible check your answers with someone who speaks English. Here are some sample answers:
1 I hate soccer.
2 I like small children.
3 I don't mind cats.
4 I have no opinion about modern art.
5 I don't like horror movies.

**70.2** 1 In my opinion violence is unnecessary.
2 I think smoking is enjoyable.
3 I'm against exams.
4 I don't think capital punishment is effective.
5 I'm in favor of nuclear power.

**70.3** 1 Apples
2 the apples
3 Women ... men
4 coffee ... tea
5 The service
6 Most people ... marriage ... family life
7 the marriage
8 the life
9 Life ... electricity
10 Skiing ... swimming
11 The Second World War
12 the people
13 art ... architecture
14 All the books
15 The beds
16 crime ... unemployment
17 violence

## Unit 71

**71.1**  1  to bed (*or* . . . I went home.)
      2  (at) home
      3  to church
      4  to school
      5  school
      6  to work
      7  in jail
      8  in college
      9  in bed

**71.2**  1  To *the* prison.    4  To *the* church.
      2  To prison.       5  To college.
      3  To school.

**71.3**  1  school
      2  school
      3  the school
      4  high school
      5  prison
      6  the prison
      7  the church
      8  church . . . church
      9  work . . . home
    10  college
    11  bed
    12  work
    13  jail

## Unit 72

**72.1**  1  wrong – Last year we visited Canada and *the* United States.
      2  right
      3  wrong – *The* south of England is warmer than *the* north.
      4  wrong – We went to Spain for our vacation and swam in *the* Mediterranean.
      5  right
      6  wrong – There are many different languages spoken in *the* Far East.
      7  wrong – Next year we are going skiing in *the* Swiss Alps.
      8  right
      9  wrong – *The* Nile is *the* longest river in Africa.
    10  wrong – *The* United Kingdom consists of Great Britain and Northern Ireland.

**72.2**  1  South America
      2  Africa
      3  *the* Philippines
      4  Sweden
      5  *the* United States
      6  *the* Soviet Union
      7  Asia
      8  *the* Rocky Mountains (*the* Rockies)
      9  *the* Pacific (Ocean)
    10  *the* Indian Ocean
    11  *the* English Channel
    12  *the* Mediterranean (Sea)
    13  *the* North Sea
    14  *the* Danube
    15  *the* Panama Canal

## Unit 73

**73.1**  1  Yes, Brown's on Cherry Road.
      2  Yes, the Park Hotel on Park Road.
      3  Yes, First National Bank on Forest Avenue.
      4  Yes, the Peking Restaurant on Cherry Road.
      5  Yes, St. Peter's (Church) on Washington Street.
      6  Yes, the City Museum on Washington Street.
      7  Yes, Riverside Park at the end of Washington Street.

**73.2**  1  the White House
      2  the Supreme Court Building . . . the Capitol Building
      3  Georgetown University
      4  Jack's
      5  O'Hare Airport
      6  The Smithsonian
      7  Luigi's
      8  the Lincoln Memorial
      9  the Sheraton
    10  the Quad
    11  Yonge Street
    12  Barclay's Bank

# Unit 74

**74.1**
1 shorts
2 a means
3 means
4 some scissors / a pair of scissors
5 a series
6 series
7 species
8 people

**74.2**
1 don't
2 was
3 wasn't
4 want
5 isn't
6 they're
7 Do
8 aren't
9 is

**74.3**
1 She was a 27-year-old woman.
2 It was a three-hour flight.
3 It was a four-day strike.
4 It is a 200-page book.
5 They were ten-year-old boys.
6 It is a ten-part television series.
7 It is a two-liter bottle.
8 They were ten-dollar tickets.
9 It is a ten-story building.
10 It is a five-pound bag of potatoes.
11 It was a five-mile walk.

# Unit 75

**75.1**
1 Tom's camera
2 the cat's eyes
3 the top of the page
4 Charles's daughter
5 today's newspaper
6 the children's toys
7 your wife's name
8 the name of this street
9 the name of the man I saw you with yesterday
10 the new manager of the company (*or* the company's new manager)
11 the result of the football game
12 Mike's parents' car
13 my father's birthday
14 the new principal of the school (*or* the school's new principal)
15 our neighbors' garden
16 the ground floor of the building
17 Don and Mary's children
18 the economic policy of the government (*or* the government's economic policy)
19 the husband of the woman talking to Tom
20 my aunt and uncle's house

**75.2**
1 *Last week's storm* caused a lot of damage.
2 *The town's only movie theater* has been closed down.
3 *Canada's exports* to the United States have fallen recently.
4 There will be a big crowd at *this evening's football game.*
5 *The region's main industry* is tourism.

**75.3**
1 ... a two weeks' vacation / 14 days' vacation
2 an hour's sleep / one hour's sleep
3 ten minutes' walk

# Unit 76

**76.1**
1 Don't *burn yourself.*
2 They had *locked themselves* out.
3 She really shouldn't *blame herself.*
4 I could *kick myself*!
5 I'm trying to *teach myself* Spanish ...
6 ... that he *talks to himself.*
7 We can *take care of ourselves.*

**76.2**
1 I really *feel* good today ...
2 ... and dried herself.
3 ... I just couldn't *concentrate.*
4 Jack and I first *met* at a party ...
5 Why don't you *relax* more?
6 We really *enjoyed ourselves* very much.
7 I didn't have time to *wash* or ...

**76.3**  1  each other (*or* one another)
      2  themselves
      3  each other (*or* one another)
      4  themselves
      5  each other (*or* one another)

**76.4**  1  I cut it myself.
      2  I went by myself.
      3  Linda told me herself. (*or* Linda herself told me.)

4  No, he types them himself. (*or* No, he does it himself.)
5  She prefers to work by herself.
6  No, I'll mail it myself. (*or* No, I'll do it myself.)
7  Why don't you clean them yourself? (*or* Why don't you do it yourself?)

---

# Unit 77

**77.1**  1  We met a relative of *yours*.
      2  Henry borrowed a book of *mine*.
      3  Tom invited some friends of *his* to his apartment.
      4  We had dinner with a neighbor of *ours*.
      5  Ann is in love with a colleague of *hers*.
      6  They went on vacation with two friends of *theirs*.
      7  I just saw a teacher of *yours*.
      8  We're spending the weekend with a friend of *ours*.
      9  We met a friend of *Jane's*.

**77.2**  1  I have *my own* television in my bedroom.
      2  They want to start *their own* business.
      3  He has / He's got *his own* private jet.
      4  . . . it has *its own* parliament and laws.
      5  We want to buy *our own* house.
      6  She has *her own* ideas.
      7  . . . he doesn't have *his own* office.

**77.3**  1  It's your own fault.
      2  Why doesn't he buy his own cigarettes?
      3  Can't you use your own pen?
      4  I usually make my own clothes.
      5  He has to cook his own meals.
      6  She rolls her own cigarettes.
      7  She has her own money.

In these sentences it is not necessary to repeat the noun. So you can also say:
      1  It's *your own*.
      2  Why doesn't he buy *his own*?
      3  Can't you use *your own*?
      4  I usually make *my own*.
      5  He has to cook *his own*.
      6  She rolls *her own*.
      7  She has *her own*.

---

# Unit 78

**78.1**  1  . . . *none of us* had an umbrella / *none of us* had brought an umbrella.
      2  They didn't tell *any of their friends*.
      3  Do you want *some of it*?
      4  *Many of the buildings* are over 800 years old.
      5  He spent / He has spent / He is going to spend *half of it* on a new car.
      6  The manager interviewed *each of the people who applied*.
      7  *Most of the people* live in the south.
      8  *Few of the members* are over 25.
      9  . . . but *none of the letters* were (*or* was) for her.

**78.2**  1  most *of*          4  Most *of*
      2  most            5  Most *of*
      3  Most            6  most *of*

**78.3**  1  Most of it.
      2  Some of them.
      3  A few of them.
      4  Most of them.
      5  All of it.
      6  Not many of them.
      7  Some of it.
      8  Not all of it.
      9  Half of it.

# Unit 79

**79.1**
1  both ... Both ... Both *of* (them)
2  Neither
3  either *of*
4  either (You could also say: "You can go *both* ways.")
5  Both (*or* both *of*)
6  Neither *of*
7  either (*or* either of them)
8  Neither
9  both *of*
10  neither *of*
11  both

**79.2**
1  The hotel was *neither* clean *nor* comfortable.
2  The movie was *both* very boring *and* very long.
3  That man's name is *either* Richard *or* Robert.
4  I have *neither* the time *nor* the money to take a vacation.
5  We can leave *either* today *or* tomorrow.
6  He gave up his job *both* because he needed a change *and* because the pay was low.
7  Laura *neither* smokes *nor* eats meat.
8  *Both* the front *and* the back of the house need painting.

# Unit 80

**80.1**
1  anyone/anybody
2  something
3  anywhere
4  anything
5  someone/somebody
6  anywhere ... anyone/anybody ... any
7  some
8  She never tells *anyone anything*. (*or* She never tells *anybody anything*.)
9  something
10  any
11  any ... some
12  anything to anyone/anybody
13  some
14  anyone/anybody
15  Anyone/Anybody
16  some
17  anywhere ... any

**80.2**
1  If *anyone/anybody* rings the doorbell, don't let them in.
2  If *anyone/anybody* asks you *any* questions, don't tell them anything.
3  If *anyone/anybody* saw the accident they should contact the police.

**80.3**
1  You can wear anything you like.
2  You can sit anywhere you like.
3  You can come any day you like.
4  You can talk to anyone/anybody you like.
5  You can travel on any flight you like.
6  You can marry anyone/anybody you like.
7  You can call (at) any time you like.

# Unit 81

**81.1**
1  Nowhere.
2  None.
3  Nothing.
4  No one / Nobody.
5  None of it.
6  I'm not going anywhere.
7  They don't have any (children).
8  I didn't dance with anyone/anybody.
9  They didn't give me anything.

**81.2**   1  anyone/anybody
       2  Nowhere
       3  no
       4  anything
       5  no one / nobody
       6  Nothing
       7  none
       8  anywhere
       9  Nothing . . . anything
     10  none
     11  No
     12  No one / Nobody . . . anything
     13  None
     14  none . . . any

**81.3**   1  I can't go *any faster*.
       2  He is *no older* than you. / He *isn't any older* than you.
       3  . . . I couldn't come *any earlier / any sooner*.
       4  Is the other one *any cheaper / any less expensive?*
       5  I can't walk *any further / any farther*.

---

# Unit 82

**82.1**   1  much ("a lot of" is also possible)
       2  a lot of
       3  much ("a lot" is also possible)
       4  a lot of . . . much
       5  A lot of ("many" is also possible)
       6  a lot of
       7  much ("a lot" is also possible)
       8  a lot of
       9  a lot of
     10  much
     11  a lot of
     12  many ("a lot of" is also possible)

**82.2**   1  He has *plenty of money*.
       2  We have / We've got *plenty of gas*.
       3  There is *plenty of room*.
       4  We have / We've got *plenty of eggs*.
       5  There are *plenty of hotels*.
       6  You've had *plenty to eat*.
       7  You have / You've got *plenty of things to do*.

**82.3**   1  *a* little      6  little
       2  *a* few       7  *a* few
       3  *a* few       8  few
       4  *a* little      9  little
       5  few

---

# Unit 83

**83.1**   1  Everyone/Everybody
       2  Everyone/Everybody . . . everything
       3  everything (*or* Her husband does *it all*.)
       4  all ("everything" is also possible)
       5  everyone/everybody
       6  All
       7  everything
       8  All
       9  everything
     10  All
     11  Everyone/Everybody

**83.2**   1  He drank the whole bottle.
       2  They searched the whole house.
       3  She worked the whole day.
       4  The whole family plays tennis.
       5  It rained the whole week.
       6  The whole building was destroyed in the fire.
       7  The whole team played well.
       8  She worked *all day*.
       9  It rained *all week*.

**83.3**   1  every four hours
       2  every four years
       3  every six months
       4  every ten minutes

# Unit 84

**84.1**  2  A burglar is someone who breaks into a
house and steals things.
3  A vegetarian is someone who doesn't
eat meat.
4  A customer is someone who buys
something from a store.
5  A shoplifter is someone who steals
from a store.
6  A pharmacist is someone who fills
prescriptions for medicine.

"That" is possible instead of "who" in
all these sentences.

**84.2**  1  The man who (*or* that) answered the
phone told me you were out.
2  The waitress who (*or* that) served us
was very impolite and impatient.

3  The b⌂
have

**84.3**  2  ..
3  ..
4  ...
5  ... who ⌐
telephone.
6  ... that (*or* which⌐
wall?
7  ... that (*or* which) was fou⌐
8  ... that (*or* which) gives you t⌐
meanings of words.
9  ... who (*or* that) are never on time.
10  ... that (*or* which) can support life.

# Unit 85

**85.1**  2  ... (that) Ann is wearing.
3  ... (that) we wanted to visit ...
4  ... (who/that) I invited to the party ...
5  ... (who/that) we met yesterday.
6  ... (that) we had for dinner ...
7  ... (that) Tom recommended.
8  ... (that) Tom tells ...
9  ... (who/that) the police arrested ...

"Which" is possible instead of "that" in 2, 3,
6, 7, and 8.

**85.2**  2  ... (that) I applied for.
3  ... (who/that) she is married to ...
4  ... (that) we went to ...
5  ... (who/that) you were with last night?
6  ... (that) we wanted to travel on ...
7  ... (who/that) I work with.

8  ... (that) they were talking about.
9  ... (that) I'm living in ...

"Which" is possible instead of "that" in 2, 4,
6, 8, and 9.

**85.3**  1  (that)
2  what
3  that (you cannot leave out "that" in this
sentence because it is the subject)
4  (that)
5  (that)
6  who/that (you cannot leave out "who"
or "that" because it is the subject)
7  (that)
8  what
9  (that)

# Unit 86

**86.1**  2  What was the name of the man whose
wife got sick and was taken to the
hospital?
3  What was the name of the woman
whose husband was arrested by the
police?
4  What was the name of the girl whose
passport was stolen?

5  What was the name of the couple
whose luggage disappeared?

**86.2**  2  ... where she had bought it.
3  ... where we can have a really good
meal?
4  ... where I can buy postcards?
5  ... where we spent our vacation ...
6  ... where people are buried.

... whose parents are dead.
... (why/that) I didn't write to
you ...
4 (that) you called.
5 ... whose dog bit me.

6 ... (why/that) they don't have a car ...
7 ... where John is staying?
8 ... (that) World War II ended.

## Unit 87

**87.1**
1 She showed me a photograph of her son, *who is a police officer.*
2 We decided not to swim in the ocean, *which looked rather dirty.*
3 The new stadium, *which holds 90,000 people,* will be opened next month.
4 Joan, *who (whom) I have known for eight years,* is one of my closest friends.
5 That man over there, *whose name I don't remember,* is an artist.
6 Opposite our house there is a nice park, *where there are some beautiful trees.*
7 The storm, *which nobody had been expecting,* caused a lot of damage.
8 The mail carrier, *who is nearly always on time,* was late this morning.
9 We often go to visit our friends in Baltimore, *which is only 30 miles away.*
10 Mr. Edwards, *whose health hasn't been good recently,* has gone into the hospital for some tests.
11 Jack looks much nicer without his beard, *which made him look much older.*
12 I went to see the doctor, *who told me to rest for a few days.*
13 Thank you for your letter, *which I was very happy to get.*
14 A friend of mine, *whose mother is the manager of a company,* helped me to get a job.
15 Next weekend I'm going to Montreal, *where my sister lives.*
16 The population of London, *which was once the largest city in the world,* is now falling.
17 I looked up at the moon, *which was very bright that evening.*
18 We spent a pleasant day by the lake, *where we had a picnic.*

## Unit 88

**88.1**
1 This is a photograph of our friends, *who* we went on vacation *with.* (*or* ... friends, *with whom* we went on vacation.)
2 The wedding, *which* only members of the family were invited *to,* took place last Friday. (*or* The wedding, *to which* only members of the family were invited, ... )
3 I've just bought some books about astronomy, *which* I'm very interested *in.* (*or* ... astronomy, *in which* I'm very interested.)

**88.2**
1 They gave us a lot of information, most of which was useless.
2 There were a lot of people at the party, only a few of whom I had met before.
3 I have sent him two letters, neither of which has arrived.
4 Norman won $50,000, half of which he gave to his parents.
5 Ten people, none of whom were qualified, applied for the job.
6 Tom made a number of suggestions, most of which were very helpful.

**88.3**
2 ... which makes it difficult to contact her.
3 ... which was perfectly true.
4 ... which means I can't leave the country.
5 ... which was very nice of him.
6 ... which I thought was very rude of them.
7 ... which makes it difficult to sleep.

# Unit 89

**89.1**
1 A plane carrying 28 passengers crashed into the ocean yesterday.
2 When I was walking home, there was a man following me.
3 I was awakened by the baby crying.
4 At the end of the street there is a path leading to the river.
5 Some paintings belonging to the artist were stolen from the gallery.

**89.2**
1 The window broken in last night's storm has now been repaired.
2 Most of the suggestions made at the meeting were not very practical.

3 The paintings stolen from the museum haven't been found yet.
4 Did you hear about the boy knocked down on his way to school this morning?

**89.3**
3 working . . . studying
4 called
5 mailed
6 waiting . . . sitting . . . reading
7 offering
8 blown
9 living

# Unit 90

**90.1**
1 a) depressing   b) depressed
2 a) interested   b) interesting
3 a) boring   b) bored
4 a) excited   b) exciting
5 a) exhausting   b) exhausted

**90.2**
1 horrified
2 embarrassing
3 interested
4 exciting
5 terrifying . . . shocked
6 amazed
7 disgusting
8 embarrassed

**90.3**
1 interested
2 tiring
3 bored . . . boring
4 boring . . . interesting
5 astonished
6 excited

# Unit 91

**91.1**
1 an unusual gold ring
2 a nice old lady
3 a good-looking young man
4 an attractive modern house
5 black leather gloves
6 an old American movie
7 a large red nose
8 a lovely sunny day
9 a nice hot bath
10 an ugly orange dress
11 a little old red car
12 a small black metal box
13 a long thin face
14 a long wide avenue
15 a big fat black cat
16 a lovely little old village
17 beautiful long blonde hair
18 an interesting old French painting

**91.2**
2 tastes awful
3 sounded . . . interesting
4 feel fine
5 smell nice
6 look wet

**91.3**
1 quietly
2 quiet
3 nice
4 well
5 safe
6 safely
7 nervous
8 slow
9 angrily

## Unit 92

**92.1**
1 wrong – nervously
2 right
3 wrong – continuously
4 wrong – happily
5 right
6 wrong – speaks very good English (*or* speaks English very well)
7 wrong – colorfully
8 right
9 wrong – terribly

**92.2**
1 patiently
2 badly
3 suspiciously
4 intentionally

5 unexpectedly
6 temporarily
7 perfectly . . . slowly . . . clearly
8 easily

**92.3**
2 seriously ill
3 fully insured (*or* completely insured)
4 absolutely enormous
5 slightly damaged
6 badly planned
7 unusually quiet (*or* extremely/completely quiet)
8 completely changed
9 extremely sorry

## Unit 93

**93.1**
1 right
2 wrong – well
3 wrong – hard
4 wrong – good
5 wrong – well
6 right
7 right

**93.2**
2 well known
3 well kept
4 well balanced
5 well informed
6 well dressed

**93.3**
1 I hardly slept last night.
2 I can hardly hear you.
3 I hardly recognized him.
4 They could hardly speak.

**93.4**
1 hardly ever
2 hardly any
3 Hardly anyone/anybody
4 hardly anywhere
5 hardly ever
6 hardly anything . . . hardly anywhere
7 hardly any

## Unit 94

**94.1**
1 so
2 such
3 such
4 so
5 such
6 such
7 so
8 such

**94.2**
1 I was so excited about going away (that) I couldn't sleep.
2 The water was so dirty (that) we decided not to go swimming.
3 She speaks English so well (that) you would think it was her native language.

**94.3**
1 It is such a narrow road (that) it is difficult for two cars to pass each other.
2 It was such warm weather (that) I didn't need a coat.
3 He has such big feet (that) he has trouble finding shoes to fit him.
4 Why do you put such a lot of sugar in your coffee?

**94.4**
1 I didn't know it was so far from your house to the airport.
2 It doesn't usually take us so long to get home (in the evening).
3 Why have you got so much furniture in this room? (*or* Why do you have . . . )

# Unit 95

**95.1**
2 enough money
3 enough cups
4 warm enough
5 enough room
6 well enough
7 enough time
8 enough qualifications
9 big enough

**95.2**
1 I'm too busy to talk to you now.
2 No, it's too late to go to the movies.
3 It's not warm enough to sit outside.
4 No, I'm too nice to be a politician.
5 No, I don't have enough money to go away on vacation this year.

6 No, it's too dark to take a picture.
7 No, we were too far away to hear what he was saying.
8 No, she doesn't speak enough English to make herself understood.
9 No, he's too lazy to work.

**95.3**
1 This coffee is too hot (for me) to drink.
2 The piano was too heavy (for *any*body) to move.
3 This coat is not warm enough (for me) to wear in winter.
4 That chair isn't strong enough (for you) to stand on.
5 This car is not big enough for six people to fit in.

# Unit 96

**96.1**
1 Our house is easy to find.
2 The window was very hard to open.
3 Some words are impossible to translate.
4 Bread is not very difficult to make.
5 That chair isn't safe to stand on.
6 Some grammatical rules are difficult to explain.
7 A good restaurant is hard to find in this town.

**96.2**
2 the first (person) to complain
3 the last person to see him
4 the first man to walk on the moon
5 the last (person) to arrive

**96.3**
2 glad to hear
3 astonished to find
4 happy to see
5 sorry to hear

**96.4**
1 It was kind of Sue to offer to help me.
2 It's careless of you to make the same mistake over and over.
3 It was stupid of her to go out in the rain without a raincoat.
4 It was nice of Don and Jenny to invite me to stay with them for a few days.
5 It wasn't polite of him to leave without saying thank you.

# Unit 97

**97.1**
2 thinner
3 more interested
4 more easily
5 quieter (*or* more quiet)
6 more crowded
7 earlier
8 more often
9 more expensive
10 nearer

**97.2**
1 longer . . . than
2 more painful than
3 older than
4 simpler than

5 more fluently than
6 more important than
7 cheaper than
8 healthier than (*or* more healthy) and more peaceful than

**97.3**
1 a little warmer today than
2 a bit more slowly
3 far more interesting than
4 much more comfortable than
5 a little happier
6 much bigger
7 a lot easier

# Unit 98

**98.1**  1  worse
2  better than
3  elder (*or* older)
4  worse than
5  further (*or* farther)
6  older (than him)
7  worse
8  further

**98.2**  1  more and more nervous
2  bigger and bigger
3  heavier and heavier
4  worse and worse
5  more and more talkative
6  more and more expensive
7  better and better

**98.3** 2–6  The longer he waited, the more impatient he became.
The more I got to know him, the more I liked him.
The more you practice your English, the faster you'll learn.
The longer the telephone call, the more you have to pay.
The more goods you sell, the more profit you'll make.

---

# Unit 99

**99.1**  1  My salary isn't as high as yours.
2  You don't know as much about cars as I do. (*or* . . . as me.)
3  I don't smoke as much as I used to.
4  I don't feel as tired as I felt yesterday. (*or* . . . as I did yesterday.)
5  They haven't lived here as long as we have. (*or* . . . as us.)
6  I wasn't as nervous before the interview as I usually am. (*or* . . . as usual.)
7  The weather isn't as bad today as it was yesterday. (*or* . . . isn't as unpleasant today . . . )

**99.2**  1  It isn't as cold today as (it was) yesterday.
2  The station wasn't as far as I thought.
3  I don't go out as much as I used to. (*or* . . . as often as I used to.)

4  The hotel isn't as expensive as I expected.
5  There weren't as many people at this meeting as (at) the last one.
6  The exam wasn't as difficult as we expected. (*or* . . . as hard as we expected.)

**99.3**  2  just as comfortable as
3  just as well-qualified as
4  just as bad as
5  just as expensive (as this one)

**99.4**  1  Your hair is the same color as mine (is).
2  I arrived here at the same time as you (did).
3  You made the same mistake as I made. (*or* . . . as me.)

---

# Unit 100

**100.1**  1  It's the cheapest restaurant in town.
2  It was the happiest day of my life.
3  She is the most intelligent student in the school.
4  It is the most valuable painting in the gallery.
5  He's one of the richest men in the world.

6  It's one of the oldest castles in France.
7  She is one of the best students in the class.
8  It was one of the worst experiences of my life. (*or* . . . in my life.)
9  He is one of the most dangerous criminals in the country.

**100.2** 1 That's the funniest story I've ever heard.
2 It's the worst mistake he's ever made.
3 That's the best coffee I've tasted in a long time.
4 This is the most uncomfortable bed I've ever slept in.
5 It's the biggest meal I've ever had.
6 Ann is the most generous person I've ever met.
7 You are the best friend I've ever had.
8 This is the most difficult decision I've had to make in years.

**100.3** 2 Who is the most famous singer in your country?
3 What is the most popular sport in your country?
4 What is the most expensive thing you have ever bought?
5 What was the happiest day of your life?
6 What is the most stupid thing you have ever done? (*or* ... stupidest thing ...)
7 Who is the most intelligent person you know?
8 Who is the most beautiful person you know?

# Unit 101

**101.1** 1 wrong – Jim doesn't like baseball very much.
2 wrong – Ann drives her car to work every day.
3 right
4 wrong – Maria speaks English very well.
5 wrong – After eating my dinner quickly, I went out.
6 wrong – You watch television all the time.
7 right
8 wrong – I think I'll go to bed early tonight.
9 right
10 wrong – I got out of bed immediately.
11 right
12 wrong – We went to the movies last night.

**101.2** 1 She won the game easily.
2 Please don't ask that question again.
3 Does Ken play tennis every weekend?

4 I closed the door quietly.
5 I remembered his name after a few minutes. (*or* After a few minutes I remembered his name.)
6 Ann writes a letter to her parents every week. (*or* Every week Ann ...)
7 Please write your name at the top of the page.
8 We found some interesting books in the library.
9 They are building a new hotel across from the park.
10 I go to the bank every Friday. (*or* Every Friday I go to the bank.)
11 Why did you come home so late?
12 I've been walking around town all morning.
13 Have you been to the theater recently?
14 I'm going to London for a few days next week.
15 I didn't see you at the party on Saturday night.

# Unit 102

**102.1** 1 right
2 wrong – ... are probably French.
3 wrong – Amy hardly ever gets angry.
4 wrong – We were both astonished ...
5 right
6 wrong – ... I also went to the bank.
7 wrong – Jim always has to hurry ...
8 right
9 wrong – I am usually very tired ...
10 right

**102.2**
1 Have you ever been arrested?
2 I don't usually have to work on Saturdays.
3 Does Tom always sing when he's taking a shower?
4 I'll probably be home late tonight.
5 We are all going away tomorrow.
6 I was only joking.
7 Did you both enjoy the party?
8 I must also write some letters.

**102.3**
1 usually take
2 has probably gone
3 is always
4 were both born
5 can also sing
6 often breaks
7 always have to wait
8 can only read ("I can read only with glasses" is also possible)
9 will probably be leaving
10 probably won't be (*or* will probably not be)
11 might never have met

## Unit 103

**103.1**
2 Is he still single?
3 Is he still working in a factory?
4 Does he still have a beard? (*or* Has he still got a beard?)
5 Does he still want to be a politician?
6 Does he still smoke a lot?

**103.2**
1 He hasn't gone yet.
2 It isn't finished yet.
3 They haven't woken up yet.
4 She hasn't come back yet. (*or* She *isn't* back yet.)
5 She hasn't gone to bed yet.
6 He hasn't replied to our letter yet.
7 I haven't decided what color to paint the wall yet. (*or* I haven't yet decided what color . . . )

**103.3**
1 He still has long hair, but he doesn't have a beard anymore. (*or* . . . he hasn't got a beard anymore.)
2 She is still in the hospital, but she isn't in critical condition anymore.
3 She is still a student, but she isn't studying economics anymore.
4 I'm still feeling tired (*or* I still feel tired), but I'm not feeling sick anymore. (*or* I don't feel sick anymore.)
5 He is a still a good player, but he isn't the best on the team anymore.
6 I still like George, but I don't like Ken anymore.
8 She is no longer in critical condition.
9 She no longer studies economics. (*or* She is no longer studying economics.)
10 I'm no longer feeling sick. (*or* I no longer feel sick.)

## Unit 104

**104.1**
2 Although I had never seen him before
3 although it was quite cold
4 although we don't like her very much
5 Although I didn't speak the language
6 although he had promised to be on time

**104.2**
1 In spite of (*or* despite)
2 Although
3 although
4 In spite of ("Despite" is also possible.)
5 in spite of ("Despite" is also possible.)
6 although

**104.3**  1  Despite his French name, he is in fact American. / Despite having a French name . . . / Despite the fact (that) he has . . .
2  Although she had an injured foot, she managed to walk home. / Although her foot was injured . . .
3  I decided to accept the job in spite of the low salary. / . . . in spite of the salary being low. / . . . in spite of the fact (that) the salary was low.
4  We lost the match despite being the better team. / . . . despite the fact (that) we were the better team.
5  Even though I hadn't eaten for 24 hours, I didn't feel hungry.

**104.4**  1  I don't like her husband though.
2  It's a bit windy though.
3  We ate it though.

# Unit 105

**105.1**  1  B: Even Sue?
A: Yes, even Sue was on time.
2  B: Even you?
A: Yes, even I make mistakes sometimes.
3  B: Even the police?
A: Yes, even the police are going on strike.
4  B: Not even his wife?
A: No, not even his wife knows where he has gone.
5  B: Even George?
A: Yes, even George passed the exam.

**105.2**  1  They even painted the floor white.
2  He even has to work on Sundays.
3  You could even hear the noise from the next street.
4  They even have the window open when it's freezing. (*or* They have the window open even when it's freezing.)
5  I can't even remember her name.
6  There isn't even a movie theater (in this town).
7  I haven't even eaten a piece of bread (today).
8  He didn't even tell his wife (where he was going).
9  I don't even know the people next door.

**105.3**  1  even cheaper
2  even better
3  even more crowded
4  even older
5  even less

# Unit 106

**106.1**  1  We smiled as we posed for the photograph.
2  I listened carefully as he explained what I had to do.
3  The crowd cheered as the two teams ran onto the field.
4  She didn't look at me as she passed me on the street.
5  It started to rain just as we arrived at the beach.
6  You moved just as I took the photograph.
7  Tom fell as he was climbing out of the window.
8  A dog ran out in front of the car as we were driving along the road.
9  She dropped her bag as she was getting out of the car.

**106.2**  2–6  As there isn't anything to eat in the house, let's go out to eat.
As it was a nice day, we decided to go for a walk.
As we didn't want to wake anyone up, we came in very quietly.
As the door was open, I walked in.
As I didn't have enough money for a taxi, I had to walk home.

## Unit 107

**107.1**  1  like       5  like       9  as
      2  like       6  As        10  like
      3  as         7  as        11  like
      4  like       8  like      12  like

**107.2**  1  like       4  as        7  as
      2  like       5  like      8  like
      3  as         6  as

**107.3**  1  like       6  as
      2  as         7  as
      3  like       8  as
      4  as         9  like (*or* such as)
      5  like      10  as

## Unit 108

**108.1**
2  He sounded as if he was calling long distance.
3  She didn't look as if she was enjoying it.
4  He smelled as if he hadn't washed in ages.
5  You look as if you've seen a ghost.
6  I feel as if I'm going to be sick.
7  She looked as if she had hurt her leg.
8  They ate their dinner as if they hadn't eaten for a week.
9  She looked as if she was going to throw it at him.

**108.2**
2  It looks as if (*or* like) it's going to rain.
3  It sounds as if (*or* like) they are having an argument.
4  It looks as if (*or* like) there's been an accident.
5  It looks as if (*or* like) we'll have to walk home.
6  It sounds as if (*or* like) you had a good time.

**108.3**
1  as if I were a child.
2  as if she knew me.
3  as if he were my boss.

## Unit 109

**109.1**
2  on July 21, 1969
3  on Saturdays
4  at night
5  at the age of five
6  in the 1920s
7  at the same time
8  in 1917
9  at the moment . . . in about five minutes

**109.2**
1  on . . . on    10  in . . . at   19  on
2  at . . . at    11  at            20  in
3  at . . . in    12  at            21  on
4  in             13  in            22  in
5  on             14  On            23  at
6  in             15  on            24  on
7  on             16  at            25  at
8  on . . . at    17  at . . . in   26  on
9  in . . . in    18  at            27  in

## Unit 110

**110.1**  1  for        5  during
      2  for        6  for
      3  during     7  during
      4  for        8  for

**110.2**  1  while      7  while
      2  While      8  during
      3  During     9  during
      4  while     10  while
      5  During    11  during
      6  while     12  while

**110.3** If possible check your answers with someone who speaks English. Here are some sample answers:
1 I fell asleep during the party.
2 The lights suddenly went out while we were having dinner.
3 I hurt my arm while I was playing tennis.

4 The students looked bored during the lecture.
5 Can you wait here while I call Tom?
6 It rained a lot during the night.
7 I fell off my chair during the interview.
8 It started to rain while we were waiting for the bus.
9 She burned herself while she was cooking.

# Unit 111

**111.1**
1 I have to be at the airport by 10:30.
2 Let me know by Saturday whether you can come to the party.
3 Please make sure that you are here by 2:00.
4 If you want to take the exam, you have to register by April 3.
5 If we leave now, we should be in Winnipeg by lunchtime.

**111.2**
| | | | |
|---|---|---|---|
| 1 | by | 4 | by |
| 2 | until | 5 | until |
| 3 | by | 6 | by |

**111.3**
1 By the time I got to the station
2 By the time the police arrived
3 By the time the guards discovered what had happened
4 By the time I finished my work

# Unit 112

**112.1**
1 on the bottle
2 at the gate
3 in an armchair . . . on the wall
4 at the top of the stairs . . . at the bottom of the stairs
5 He's looking (at himself) in the mirror.
6 on the third floor
7 in the back of the car
8 in the back (*or* in the back row)
9 on the left . . . on the right
10 on the door
11 at/on the corner (of the street)
12 in the corner (of the room)

**112.2**
2 on the right
3 on my way to work
4 in the Swiss Alps

5 on the west coast
6 at the window
7 on the third floor
8 on the front page of the newspaper
9 in the front row
10 in the back of the class
11 on the back of the envelope

**112.3**
| | | | |
|---|---|---|---|
| 1 | at/on | 10 | on |
| 2 | on | 11 | in |
| 3 | at | 12 | on |
| 4 | in | 13 | on . . . on |
| 5 | in . . . in | 14 | in |
| 6 | At | 15 | on |
| 7 | at | 16 | on |
| 8 | in | 17 | on |
| 9 | in . . . on | | |

# Unit 113

**113.1**
2 in bed
3 at the movie theater
4 in prison
5 on a farm
6 in school

7 at the National Theatre
8 in the hospital
9 at sea
10 at the airport

| 113.2 | 1 | at | 7 | at | | 113.3 | 1 | in | 6 | at |
|---|---|---|---|---|---|---|---|---|---|---|
| | 2 | at | 8 | at | | | 2 | at | 7 | in |
| | 3 | in | 9 | at (*or no preposition*) | | | 3 | in | 8 | at |
| | 4 | at work . . . at | | . . . at | | | 4 | at | 9 | in |
| | | home . . . in bed | 10 | in | | | 5 | arrive home | 10 | arrived home |
| | 5 | at | 11 | at | | | | (*no preposition*) | | (*no preposition*) |
| | 6 | at | | | | | | | | |

---

# Unit 114

**114.1**
1 to
2 going home (*no preposition*)
3 by . . . on
4 to . . . get home (*no preposition*)
5 on
6 on
7 by
8 to
9 into
10 to
11 in

**114.2**
1 Have you been to Africa?
2 Have you been to Japan?
3 Have you been to Rome?
4 Have you been to Moscow?
5 Have you been to Canada?
6 Have you been to Puerto Rico?

If possible check your sentences for numbers 7–10 with someone who speaks English. Here are some sample anwers:

7–10 I've been to Canada many times.
I've never been to Puerto Rico.
I've been to Moscow once.
I've been to Japan three times.

**114.3**
1 I got on the bus.
2 I got out of the car.
3 I got off the train.
4 I got in/into the taxi.
5 I got off my bike . . .

---

# Unit 115

**115.1**
1 a solution *to* the problem
2 a good relationship *with* her brother
3 a big increase *in* prices
4 an answer *to* your question
5 no demand *for* shoes like these anymore
6 some advantages *in* being married ("advantages *to* being married" is also possible)
7 a fall *in* the number of people without jobs this year
8 any need *for* a new highway

**115.2**
1 to
2 of
3 of
4 to
5 for . . . in
6 between
7 for
8 of
9 for
10 of
11 in (*or* to)
12 in
13 to
14 with
15 of
16 to
17 to
18 for
19 with
20 toward
21 to

---

# Unit 116

**116.1**
2 on strike
3 by mistake
4 for breakfast
5 on television
6 on time
7 in love
8 for a swim
9 on business
10 by check
11 on a diet
12 in time
13 on the phone
14 by Shakespeare

**116.2**
1 for
2 in . . . out
3 for
4 in
5 by
6 on
7 on
8 for
9 for
10 on
11 on
12 pay in cash (*or* pay cash – *no preposition*
13 by
14 on
15 on
16 in
17 by
18 on
19 on
20 on
21 in

# Unit 117

**117.1** 1 I'm worried about him.
2 I'm angry with him.
3 I'm jealous of him.
4 I'm afraid of him.
5 I'm fed up with him.

**117.2**
| 1 | of | 9 | of |
|---|---|---|---|
| 2 | to . . . to | 10 | with |
| 3 | of | 11 | about |
| 4 | to | 12 | shocked *at/by* |
| 5 | about | | . . . ashamed *of* |
| 6 | with . . . for | 13 | to |
| 7 | with | 14 | at/by |
| 8 | at/by | 15 | with |

| 16 | of | 18 | to |
|---|---|---|---|
| 17 | about ("by" is also possible) | 19 | of |

**117.3** If possible check your sentences with someone who speaks English. Here are some sample answers:
1–2 *see examples*
3 I'm very good at remembering people's names.
4 I'm brilliant at telling jokes.
5 I'm pretty good at languages.

# Unit 118

**118.1**
2 short of
3 interested in
4 similar to
5 different from ("different than" is also possible in informal use)
6 capable of
7 full of
8 impressed with/by
9 tired of
10 responsible for

**118.2**
| 1 | about | 10 | with/by |
|---|---|---|---|
| 2 | of | 11 | of |
| 3 | with | 12 | in |
| 4 | of | 13 | to |
| 5 | for | 14 | from ("than" is also possible in informal use) |
| 6 | about | 15 | for |
| 7 | for | 16 | of |
| 8 | in | 17 | about |
| 9 | of | | |

# Unit 119

**119.1**
| 2 | crashed into | 6 | depends on |
|---|---|---|---|
| 3 | belong to | 7 | die of |
| 4 | Concentrate on | 8 | believe in |
| 5 | applied for | | |

| 9 | of | 12 | into |
|---|---|---|---|
| 10 | of | 13 | to |
| 11 | with | 14 | on (*or* "depends how I feel" – *no preposition*) |

**119.2**
| 1 | about | 5 | for |
|---|---|---|---|
| 2 | to . . . about | 6 | into |
| 3 | on | 7 | on |
| 4 | to | 8 | in |

**119.3**
| 1 | for | 4 | about |
|---|---|---|---|
| 2 | about | 5 | of |
| 3 | of | 6 | for |

# Unit 120

**120.1**
| 2 | happened to | 6 | rely on |
|---|---|---|---|
| 3 | listen to | 7 | laughing at |
| 4 | glanced at | 8 | live on |
| 5 | paid for | | |

**120.2**
| 1 | to | 4 | about |
|---|---|---|---|
| 2 | to | 5 | for |
| 3 | of | 6 | pay the bill (*no preposition*) |

| 7 | on | 14 | from |
|---|---|---|---|
| 8 | at | 15 | about |
| 9 | on | 16 | of |
| 10 | with | 17 | at |
| 11 | about | 18 | for |
| 12 | from | 19 | after |
| 13 | of | 20 | for |

# Unit 121

**121.1**
1  for
2  to ("with" is possible)
3  for
4  at
5  to
6  write *to* her parents ("write her parents" is also possible) . . . she calls them (*no preposition*)
7  to ("with" is possible)
8  from
9  for
10  to ("with" is possible)
11  discuss what happened (*no preposition*)
12  call the restaurant (*no preposition*)

13  about
14  of
15  of/about
16  of
17  of/about
18  of
19  about
20  of/about
21  of

**121.2**
2  I wrote to Ann *or* I wrote Ann (*no preposition*)
3  phoned (*no preposition*)
4  discussed (*no preposition*)
5  waited for
6  entered (*no preposition*)

# Unit 122

**122.1**
1  for
2  to
3  on
4  at
5  of
6  with
7  from
8  into
9  for
10  about

**122.2**
1  Ann blamed Jim *for* what happened.
2  You always blame everything *on* me.
3  Do you blame the government *for* the economic situation?
4  I blame the increase in violent crime *on* television.

5  Do you think that the government *is to blame for* the economic situation?
6  I think that television *is to blame for* the increase in violent crime.

**122.3**
1  Can you explain this question to me?
2  Can you explain the system to me?
3  Can you explain to me how this machine works?
4  Can you explain to me why English prepositions are so difficult?

# Unit 123

**123.1**
1  I prefer classical music to rock music.
2  He has a bodyguard to protect him from (*or* against) his enemies.
3  Sue provided me with all the information I needed.
4  This morning I spent $60 on a pair of shoes.
5  Ann reminded Tom about his appointment with Mr. Fox.

**123.2**
1  to
2  from/against
3  as
4  on
5  of
6  about
7  of
8  with
9  about
10  to
11  at
12  to
13  into
14  to
15  on
16  at
17  of
18  from . . . into
19  about

# Unit 124

**124.1**
3  take off
4  closed down
5  moving in
6  grows up
7  turn up
8  clears up (*or* will clear up)
9  show off
10  speak up

**124.2**
1  I put it out.
2  I took them off.
3  I turned it on.
4  I called her up.

5  I gave it up.
6  I put them on.
7  I wrote it down.

**124.3**
2  picked it up
3  wake them up
4  cross it out
5  tried it on
6  looked them up
7  shaved it off
8  knocked me out